Choosing the Witness Self

Illuminating the Illusions of the Ego Mind

Dr Talia Steed

First published by Busybird Publishing 2025.
Copyright © 2025 Talia Steed.

ISBN:
Paperback: 978-1-923501-13-3
Ebook: 978-1-923501-14-0

This work is copyright. Apart from any use permitted under the *Copyright Act 1968*, no part of this publication may be reproduced, stored in a retrieval system or transmitted in any form or by any means, electronic, mechanical, photocopying, recording or otherwise, without the prior written permission of Talia Steed.

The information in this book is based on the author's experiences and opinions. The author and publisher disclaim responsibility for any adverse consequences, which may result from use of the information contained herein. Permission to use any external content has been sought by the author. Any breaches will be rectified in further editions of the book.

Cover Image: AdobeStock_1220640872

Cover design: Busybird Publishing

Layout and typesetting: Busybird Publishing

Busybird Publishing
2/118 Para Road
Montmorency, Victoria
Australia 3094
www.busybird.com.au

All rights reserved. Without limiting the rights under copyright reserved, no part of this publication may be reproduced, stored or introduced into a retrieval system, or transmitted in any form or by any means (electronic, mechanical, photocopying, recording or otherwise) without the prior written permission of both the copyright owners and the publisher of this book. The author does not provide medical advice or prescribe the use of any technique as a form of treatment for mental health or medical problems without the advice of a physician. The intent of the author is only to offer information to help you in your quest for emotional wellbeing. In the event you use any of the information in this book for yourself, the author and the publisher assume no responsibility. The names of the participants in the stories are altered to respect their privacy.

*Transcending the stories we create in our mind,
the layers of ego and suffering, to uncover
the truth of who we really are.*

Dr Talia Steed

The Author

Dr Talia Steed MBBS

Mantra to live by: "Life is a daring adventure or it is nothing." – **Helen Keller**

Passions: spiritual literature and teachings, beach days, Sundays, camping with my love, deep conversations, laughing with my mother, yoga, dancing, writing.

Life purpose: to constantly seek to be the truest version of myself and to let go everything that is not who I am. To be of service. To spread compassion. To teach by example.

Praise for Choosing the Witness Self

Choosing the Witness Self provides thought-provoking questions, which require the reader to dive deep into an ocean of introspection, and self-reflection. The material challenges the reader to question their thought processes, their willingness to heal/explore the egoic, shadow parts of themselves, whilst trying to integrate a sense of balance in life.

Dr Steed aptly expresses her own past challenges in a relatable way, that leads one to shed light on the darkness of their own shadows. She leads us on a self-explorative journey, encouraging us all to hold our own shadows with curiosity, compassion and empathy, shifting away from self-judgement and shame. It explores the deep challenges of life, as we navigate the tug-of-war moments between our spiritual selves, and our physical selves. *Choosing the*

Witness Self will challenge your soul's identity and be the catalyst for reconnecting to the peaceful parts within you, whilst recognising that we are all "equal parts human and soul".

Tamarin Oblowitz
Clinical Psychologist, Spiritual & Holistic Therapist

Dr Talia Steed's latest book, *Choosing the Witness Self*, is the raw, vulnerable and deeply personal story of her life's path, and how a profound healing and conscious awareness of her divine inner soul essence was unearthed through many challenges and difficulties. This beautiful work bravely lays bare the author's self, whilst probing into the endless questions of the mind and the conflict of the ego-self, through deep introspection and poignant poetry – the poetry of a seeker and a soul revealed.

Layer upon layer of uncovered spiritual wisdom, like the proverbial onion, peel from the pages. You will find yourself echoed, held and supported here as you pilgrim with Dr Talia – as she first guides you through her journey and then prompts you to journal and dive deep into your own experiences.

An utterly relatable book for all and a must-read for anyone who has been wearied by walking the path of healing and spiritual seeking.

Elaine MacLeod
Holistic Energy Healer and Meditation Guide

Contents

The Author i
Praise for Choosing the Witness Self iii
Foreword 1
Acknowledgments 3

One	Vision Creates Reality....................................... 5
Two	My New Story.. 10
Three	Making Peace with Being a Human................... 25
Four	Following the Stepping Stones.......................... 35
Five	Yearning to Surrender....................................... 40
Six	Trusting the Intuitive Voice Within 51
Seven	Being Honest with Yourself............................... 63
Eight	When Enough's Enough................................... 70
Nine	Light and Love and Being Unf*ckwithable......... 78
Ten	Finding the Love of Your Life........................... 84
Eleven	The Greatest Opponent You Will Ever Face....... 92
Twelve	Writing Your Own Story.................................. 98

About the Author.. 107
Final Dedication 109

Foreword

I had the privilege of meeting Dr Talia Steed early in her writing journey. She wasn't sure if her story and struggles were worth sharing. As her mentor, I witnessed her amazing transformation as she bridged the gap between Western medicine and holistic well-being. Through this journey her first book, *Body Wisdom: What is Your Body Trying to Tell You?* was published.

In her second book, Dr Steed bravely shares her personal journey with honesty and vulnerability. She recounts her battles with physical and mental suffering, and her relentless pursuit of inner peace and life's purpose. Her courage and determination are truly inspiring.

Within the pages of this book, you will embark on a transformative journey alongside Dr Steed. Her raw and unfiltered account will take you deep into her experiences, exploring the depths of her emotions and fears, and revealing the power of healing and personal growth.

Her story will guide you to listen to your intuition and connect with your true self.

Dr Steed's narrative reminds us of the importance of embracing our struggles and the healing process. She shows us that finding inner peace and purpose is not a straightforward path, but a winding journey with its ups and downs. By facing our shadows and embracing discomfort, we can experience profound transformation.

Self-compassion is another vital aspect of Dr Steed's account. She emphasises the need to accept and love ourselves with kindness and understanding. Her story becomes a guiding light, leading us towards finding our inner peace and life's true purpose.

As you read this powerful narrative, be fully present and open to its messages. Allow Dr Steed's words to resonate with your own story, guiding you to a deeper connection with your authentic self. May her journey inspire you to listen to your intuition and embark on your own transformative path of self-discovery, knowing that the greatest treasures lie within you.

Dr Talia Steed, a remarkable individual whose courage knows no bounds, bares her soul in this heartfelt narrative and is someone I truly admire.

With gratitude and anticipation,

Iggy Tan
BSc MBA GAICD
CEO, Rotarian and Author

Acknowledgments

Sometimes there is a greater force behind a project, an idea, or a creation, greater than what the human mind can grasp or even hope to understand.

It is this that I wish to acknowledge for my second book, that rather than being created by me, was indeed created through me.

You see, when we connect with the deepest part of ourselves – the divine essence, our witness consciousness – we can access our part of the collective interconnected consciousness of all that is. And it is from this space, from this divine realm of pure consciousness, that we gain access to a wisdom far beyond the limitations of our human mind.

I believe that this journey that is accessible to each one of us – to look within and connect with the deepest parts of ourselves – not only benefits the individual self, but contributes to the evolution of the collective human consciousness.

When each one of us sheds yet another layer of our conditioned mind, gains a new awareness, or learns a deeper truth about our self – taking action to shift entrenched patterns of behaviour, thought or emotions – it leads to a ripple of positive change.

Our greatest achievements are not to be found in the external world in which we are blessed to inhabit, but in those silent moments of solitude. Those moments in which we forge a new path, choose a new direction, and work towards become a truer and freer version of ourselves. It is these shifts that we make on the inside, which few if any other human beings are privileged to bear witness to, that are truly our most valuable contributions to the world.

So I acknowledge the deepest part of you – the essence and truth of who you really are – for all you have endured, and for all you have transcended. I acknowledge your strength, your courage and the light within your soul that enables you to keep stepping forward with courage and bravery, as you face your unique challenges, that are a part of every human life.

Namaste, Dr Talia.

One

Vision Creates Reality

Our life in the external world begins with the vision we hold for it within. In relation to a health issue, when people cannot see a version of themselves free from an illness or chronic symptoms, it manifests as an endless cycle of suffering.

At one point during my time working in general practice, I asked some of my patients who had been experiencing chronic health issues, "Can you imagine a vision of yourself in the future free of this?" They paused, thought about it, and replied with a genuine sense of hopelessness. That no, they could not see a time when they could be free of what was burdening them.

Unfortunately, the chance of things getting any better is very low, if we cannot even begin to imagine it. To help shift these patients' perspectives, I started by asking them to start with something really small. Maybe they could just begin to contemplate the possibility of being able to visualise a happier and healthier self.

Our beliefs related to our health and wellbeing, or lack thereof, determine our future state of being. Although many people say that they want to feel better, the ego self, or smaller aspect of us, can keep us trapped in a vicious cycle of suffering. The negative health issues we face – be they mental, emotional or physical – in some way serve us. To achieve any real, sustainable change, we need to develop the awareness to see ourselves in our totality.

Carolyn Myss talks about the will to live versus the will to heal. Having worked in medical practice I certainly saw this to be true. Most human beings carry a will to live. Perhaps even people who continue to live with suicidal thoughts carry this will, albeit subconsciously, and it is this that helps to keep them alive.

However, the will to heal is a different story. True healing requires us to really face what has made us "sick". This may be in a major way, like a cancer diagnosis or the loss of a limb, or in a chronic, relentless way, like gut issues, chronic pain or anxiety.

In all cases, the healing process is similar. Asking oneself the question, "What has made my body, mind and spirit system so out of balance to develop these symptoms?" can be very confronting for most people. Sometimes we don't want to hear the answer, for this may require us to make changes in our lives that we are simply not ready to make.

Vision Creates Reality

To heal, we need to connect more deeply with our innermost self, and uncover the hidden messages our body is trying to communicate with us. And sometimes healing is the cure or resolution of the symptoms or disease, whilst other times it is not. Making peace and accepting our life circumstances, is also part of the healing.

However, if we are to embark on the journey to heal – in whatever shape that takes for our particular life situation – we are making a commitment to embark on a path of self-exploration that in actual fact has no end. By following this path, we choose to make a lifelong commitment to ourselves. To listen to the messages from within our own soul, rather than being governed by those that we hear from the outside world.

And this is a process that takes much practice. Much time. Much dedication. And much surrender.

So it is clear why so many people make detours away from the path of healing, or in truth don't carry the will to heal at all. For if there is a secondary gain from an illness or symptom – like not having to work, or a sickness benefit, or maintaining a relationship, or being liked by keeping others happy – some people may not wish to change that. For if healing meant giving up the things they were keeping by being sick, would they really choose to give them up?

So the question to really ask yourself is this. Is your will to heal as strong as your will to live? Or have you resigned yourself to your current life circumstances?

And if you really stop to think about it, how do you wish to spend your precious days here on this Earth?

If life flies in an instant, and if money is something you can't take with you when you go, what is it that you are waiting for?

Pearls of Wisdom:

- The vision for our lives, which our higher self holds within, creates the external world that we call into physical reality. Whether that comes as an image, a thought, a feeling, or an inner knowing.
- The only way to truly heal, is to surrender wholeheartedly to a greater purpose for our lives. This will support us in the process of letting go people, circumstances and patterns, that no longer serve us.

Vision Creates Reality

Wisdom Within:

1. What is the vision I hold for my life?

2. How do I wish to feel in my life? Can I cultivate these feelings from within, even before the things I want in the external world manifest into physical form?

3. What could be getting in the way of my vision becoming my reality?

4. What is my next right move to create the vision of my life that I desire?

Two

My New Story

There came a point at which I realised that I had been the creator of my own suffering. I had thus far surrendered my power to my ego, which had convinced me that it was not possible to be free from obsessive and compulsive thinking.

I believed that although I had made significant shifts in managing an eating disorder, depression, and anxiety, the entrenched patterns of rumination seemed like a level beyond that which I would be able to transcend. I felt powerless to change this. Like a victim to the dominance and strength of my own mind, leaving me at times feeling afraid of this negative, fear-provoking entity living in my very own head.

Yet at this turning point I saw through the illusion of this belief being true. It was just my ego at play once again, keeping me stuck in suffering to stay with what was known, preventing me from enjoying the life I had worked so hard to create. The unknown just seemed too scary to invite in and wholeheartedly embrace as my life.

So began the writing of my new story. I realised that it was possible to shift the mental processes of my brain, or at least learn how to respond to them differently. I had surmounted far greater challenges, and I was a determined and fiery spirit!

The process of shifting our mental processes and responses to them starts with awareness, for we cannot change that which we do not yet know or even see. So I started to cultivate minute-by-minute awareness of these thoughts in my head. As soon as I didn't like the trajectory of a thought, I simply said, "No thank you." It was as simple as that. No more fighting, no more antagonising, no more resisting or constricting around these thought patterns that had been so deeply laid down as neural pathways in my brain. Rather, I accepted and then gently declined them, before allowing their spiral to nowhere.

And then they returned. Boy, did they return! With a vengeance like I could never have imagined in my very worst nightmares.

I went down a well, a deep dark whirlpool of what seemed like complete insanity. Looping thoughts going round and round and round and round and round … on repeat. On repeat. On repeat. On repeat. They were relentless, fuelling the fear already lying dormant in my still sensitised nervous system from past challenges and life experiences. Perhaps even from lifetimes past, or ancestral traumas lying deep within the fibres of my DNA.

What I discovered was that underneath intrusive or ruminating streams of thought though, often lie feeling states that can be difficult to sit with. So what emotions were these loops keeping me from seeing, hiding just beneath their surface? Why was I so stressed out? Why was my mind so ill at ease?

These were the questions that required further exploration. More inner work. Just when I thought I had done enough. Ha! The spiritual journey is not for the fainthearted.

> *Broken record on repeat. Round and round and round and round you go. I try and stop you. And you just get louder.*
>
> *Loop d' loop.*
>
> *Can't I have a moment's rest?*
>
> *Dark thoughts. Why me?*
>
> *Honestly, won't it ever end?*
>
> *Thought. Neutralise. Thought. Neutralise.*
>
> *Thought. Thought. Thought. Thought.*
>
> *Drain.*

My New Story

Tried so hard. Fought and resisted with all my might.

Round and round and round you go.

How can I have achieved so much with the loop d' loop of thought replaying constantly in my head?

Can't I have a break?

A break?

A break!

Time has come.

Time to stop the fight.

Surrender. Completely surrender.

Watch the battle.

Withdraw the energy. Let it burn itself out.

Not me. Not me. So not me.

Universe, show me the way.

I am listening.

I am aware.

I am following your call.

Surely you will answer mine?

Through hypnotherapy, I uncovered buried memories from the past, that were in part connected to these thoughts. Memories with a common theme of feeling out of control, bullied, taken advantage of and on edge! Through this awareness I began the process of learning to calm down my nervous system. Repeating new mantras in my mind that I was safe, that I was in control, and that I was strong. I also knew that there was something linked between letting these thoughts invade my mind – intrusive, unpleasant and distressing that they were – and having been a person who had allowed other people to similarly invade my life.

Enough was enough! It was time for me to reclaim my life, my mind and my self. Through hypnotherapy I had discovered a way of creating a new story, by training my mind to tell my body something new.

In the process of expanding the mind to believe a new story and cultivate a new reality, we can help to calm the body, reducing or eliminating associated physical symptoms. Through illuminating our entrenched beliefs, we can seek to remove layers of our conditioning, to make closer contact with our soul essence within and our divine witness consciousness.

So the real question to ask yourself is, what old story are you listening to on repeat? What is it that needs to go from your life?

And have you reached the point at which you are tired of living a Groundhog Day life and ready to create your new story?

My New Story

There are many healing modalities out there, created to help cultivate a new version of your life. Ultimately, the most important thing to do is to follow whatever or whomever calls out to you. The modalities themselves are less important than the connection and energy exchange that happens between oneself and the person who delivers them. You will meet the right teacher you need at each point on the journey to changing your life. When you start to see that it is this that is more important than the acupuncture, herbs or style of reiki someone practices, there will be less pressure on making the right decision on who to see – and you will be guided more quickly to whom you are meant to meet.

However, one of the useful tools I discovered along my journey is hypnotherapy, which may or may not resonate for you. This was Marisa Peer's Rapid Transformational Therapy (RTT), which uses a combination of hypnosis with regression techniques to uncover any underlying memories connected with the symptom bothering you.

If this is something that you aren't drawn to, you can instead experiment with self-hypnosis if that resonates more. Or there will be something else that calls out to your soul.

In self-hypnosis, the first step is in gaining an awareness of the current belief that you are trying to change. For example, a belief that I carried for an extremely long period of time was that "I always take on the energy of other people". As an empath, holding on to this belief came at an extreme cost. It meant that I continued to take on more and more of other people's stuff – physically, mentally, emotionally and energetically! How exhausting! I became reluctant to engage with others, for fear of becoming drained and taking something on.

When I finally realised how entrenched this belief had become within the crevices of my psyche, again I decided enough is enough! I would become an empowered empath and stop taking on everything I encountered from the outside world.

It was time to expand my mind, to believe a new story, and to tell my body a new message.

Self-hypnosis for Empath Energy Boundaries
(Inspired by the work of Marisa Peer)

Okay Talia, just relax.

You have nowhere to go and nothing to do.

Just bring your entire being, into this present moment.

Keeping your eyes open, I want you to look up, look up to the space between your eyes, noticing the flickering of your eyelids, taking a big breath in and breathing everything out.

Just keep looking up, noticing that flickering, breathing in and breathing everything out.

My New Story

And when you're ready, gently close down your eyes, but keep your eyes looking up, breathing in and breathing everything out.

Now just allow your eyes to become heavy, droopy, glued shut, sealed shut. And the harder you try to open your eyes the more they become heavy, droopy, glued shut, sealed shut.

Now just forget all about your eyes.

And imagine that you are at the top of a flight of 10 steps that you are slowly going to walk down.

You take step 10, going deeper and deeper into your subconscious mind.

Step 9, your whole body becoming so deeply relaxed.

Step 8, breathing in and breathing everything out.

Step 7, going deeper and deeper.

Step 6, so completely relaxed.

Step 5, 4, 3, 2, 1.

So calm, so relaxed, safe, and completely at peace.

At the bottom of the stairs, just imagine a beam of light coming down through your crown and encircling your entire body.

Dr Talia Steed

Protecting you. Supporting you. Energising you.

You have been taking on far too much, for far too long, and it is time to create a new story for your life.

You are now an empowered empath.

You choose when to plug in and you choose when to unplug.

You stay in your own energy and you let everything else wash over you.

You are energised from the light above, and grounded and supported from the Earth below.

And if you do happen to take in something that is not yours, you are now able to quickly transmute it and send it up into the light, leaving you feeling light, unburdened and free.

So just go deeper just for a few more moments.

Know that you are light, you feel light and you emanate light.

And as you move about your days ahead, instead of letting the outside world extinguish the flame of your inner being, see your light bringing brightness and joy, to whomever you encounter on your travels through life.

I'm going to count now from 1 to 5, and on the count of 5 you will gently come back to your body feeling wide awake, completely energised and alive, and ready to move on with your day.

1, 2, 3, 4, 5. And when you are ready you can open your eyes, feeling energised, feeling alive and feeling completely protected, as the empowered empath that you are.

This is something you can write out for yourself, incorporating what you believed before, and what you would like to call in as your new way of being. You can record it and listen to it as many times as you like, until you feel that it has taken hold as a new belief in your mind. RTT practitioners talk about a minimum of 21 days, but sometimes beliefs that have been entrenched for a long time may need to be listened to for longer. Also, we may naturally find ourselves listening to the meditation every second day, or whenever we feel called to revisit it.

The OCD thoughts however, taught me that although this modality may be one way, it is by no means the only way – there is no such thing! There is no one miracle cure for each person's problems, or each of our very own problems. Hypnotherapy was extremely powerful at releasing some of the stored emotions in my body, related to my bowel's ability to release. However, when it came to the OCD, I needed to go even further.

I also subsequently found that when presented with a major series of triggers in the outside world, after five months of regular physical release, my bowels stopped working again. This doesn't discount the power of hypnotherapy – sometimes it will "work" and at other times it won't, depending on the confounding factors impacting our life situation at the time.

However, we come to realise that the circumstances that present themselves along our journey, are exactly what we need to shed yet another layer of our conditioned smaller self. The hypnotherapy gave me five months of evidence that there was really nothing wrong with my physical body, and that I could actually go to the toilet.

And it was through this experience that I came to learn just how powerful fear in the mind can be. The fears I carried about the physical symptoms, only served to perpetuate a negative cycle of being unable to have a bowel motion without a laxative tea. However, this experience was my greatest teacher in the mind–body connection, and learning how to tame the fears that held my being captive.

Through hypnotherapy, we can aim to expand the mind to reshape our beliefs and create the life we want, which is incredibly powerful. But my journey through OCD and the relapse of bowel symptoms, showed me that even the belief of being able to control the mind creates resistance in the being, which can perpetuate the symptoms we are trying to let go of. When we ignore or resist our shadow side, our negativity, or our unhelpful engrained patterns of thought or behaviour, eventually they find a way of coming out through physical symptoms or life circumstances.

Instead of bypassing the shadow, we can work towards integrating it. By developing an attitude of acceptance of whatever comes up – whatever thought, feeling or bodily sensation we become aware of – we can connect with that part of us that is beyond the mind. As a result, we will suffer less when we are less attached to pleasure, or positive experiences and emotions, and less averse to pain, or negative experiences and emotions. And as we go deeper with this, we may even start to let go of the judgements of positive and negative, simply watching whatever presents across the screen of our conscious awareness.

Sometimes we will be able to reshape old beliefs – to manifest our desires, to transmute old outdated ways of being that have kept us stuck – but other times we may not. We may get stuck in looping thoughts, we may engage with old depressive thinking, we may get anxious, activate our fears, or self-sabotage.

In these instances, the goal isn't to blame or condemn ourselves for not being spiritual enough, for not having done enough work, or for not controlling our thoughts enough, but instead to watch it. Watch it all play out. Notice the negative thinking. Notice the intrusive thoughts. And just be. Be with whatever appears across the screen of our consciousness – without fear of the content of the thoughts, the quality of the emotions, or the character of the physical sensations. Without self-blame, condemnation or guilt. With pure acceptance and curiosity. Just noticing.

In this way of being, we can make contact with pure awareness. Awareness beyond the thoughts, beyond the feelings, beyond the sensations in the body. And this is the essence of spirituality. Discovering that you are the witness to the experiences of your life. Nothing more, and nothing less.

So let go of the pressure.

You are doing your best.

Not even the most enlightened human being on this planet will never have an unpleasant thought. No one will never feel sad, or alone, or afraid.

We are all connected in the humanness of our experience here on Earth.

It is time for us to drop the pressure.

Drop the fight.

Simply notice.

Finally free.

Fearlessly observe.

And simply see, what you see.

My New Story

Pearls of Wisdom:

- Old belief patterns can keep us stuck, until they are brought into the light of our conscious awareness.
- We have the choice to let go of the old beliefs and create something new, or live a life on repeat.
- Self-hypnosis is a way that we can train ourselves to believe something new.
- RTT is a more in-depth way of clearing deep and stuck emotions, patterns of behaviour, or beliefs out of our subconscious mind, to liberate us in the present, and live the life that we deserve.
- Sometimes patterns of thoughts, feelings and beliefs will emerge that we have no option but to simply let be. To watch. To sit with. To accept.
- Resistance equals persistence.
- Acceptance equals transcendence.
- Things may be exactly as they always were, but now we watch them through an attitude of curious awareness.
- We are equal parts human and spirit. We are not here to become perfect, we are here to connect more and more deeply with the divine conscious awareness within.
- It doesn't matter what we see. Just that we notice who sees.

Wisdom Within:

1. What old belief am I carrying that it's time to release?

2. What do I need to do to help me clear this old belief, and bring in something new?

3. How can I connect more deeply with my observer self? What activities, practices, places or people, help me connect with my true/higher self?

4. Is there something I need to let go resisting, and instead bring in an attitude of acceptance towards?

Three

MAKING PEACE WITH BEING A HUMAN

The day came when I realised just how much I had been resisting being a human. To some this may sound completely absurd, as the majority of human beings are very connected with their physical form, their body, their status, their human personality.

At this stage of my journey however, I felt quite different. Yet I came to discover that there were other people who felt similarly. For a long time I had felt this displaced sense of self – that I was in the human world, but not of it. That I was floating somewhere above my life, above the interactions with others, not quite grounded in my physical form.

I had been much more connected with my soul essence, creating an uneasy and unsettled feeling within me, as I went about my daily life. A feeling of ambivalence about being present here on Earth. It's like I saw the beauty and felt the awe and magic of life, yet was so aware of the heaviness and density of human suffering, that I wanted on some level to escape and leave it all behind. Perhaps. Or perhaps it was my own suffering that resonated with what I was perceiving, that prompted the need to dissociate from the everyday stressors of human life.

Yet there came a day when I knew with much greater certainty, that it was time for me to truly accept and embrace my humanness – my emotions, my physical form, and the imperfections of all the people in my life, including myself. It was time for me to drop my judgements of myself and others, to let go of my impossible standards, and to open up to the richness and complexity of life here on Earth.

The placement of such a spiritual soul in the world of Western medicine was no accident. I knew a life purpose of mine was linked to integrating the two worlds – forming a bridge between science and spirituality.

It was time to embody my soul essence here on Earth. To show how even a super-spiritual, esoteric air sign, could live a grounded and embodied life. To connect people with the divine feminine and the divine masculine that live within each one of us, integrating these seeming polarities. To show the importance of finding the middle ground, the balance point. A meeting point of apparent opposites in the external world – and at the same time, within our inner worlds.

I knew the damage that could be caused when either was over-valued. I had seen Western medical doctors and esteemed spiritual healers similarly, often unintentionally, cause additional pain and suffering for those seeking their advice or healing guidance. This was the result of their own ego patterns getting in the way, with their unfiltered biases being projected on those seeking their counsel.

It was through these experiences that I realised the humanness of us all, and that no modality was immune from corruptive forces. This reinforced just how important it was to always maintain an attitude of discernment, especially when on a healing path. Cultivating a delicate balance between having an open mind, and only taking on what resonates for oneself from what other people have to say. Under the title of being a doctor, many doctors have unintentionally caused significant shame to their patients, by downplaying their experiences, symptoms and inner knowings. At the same time I have seen spiritual healers unintentionally traumatise vulnerable people, through instilling their own fears or biases, as a result of not remaining an impartial vessel. In either role, the effect of plugging in to others' beliefs and thought processes in a negative way, can be equally harmful.

Ultimately, no one knows us better than we know ourselves. That is truth. At the same time, sometimes others can observe aspects of ourselves that we cannot yet see, which remain outside of our conscious awareness. But the deep knowing of what is happening within our body – of what is or isn't right for us at any given moment – that inner wisdom can only come from within.

This led to the realisation, that in order to prevent myself unintentionally inflicting suffering on others as a result of my spiritual perspective for what happens in life, I had to find the middle ground. To learn to embrace not only the esoteric, the sublime, the spiritual and the magical, but also the humanness. The messy, complex, imperfect parts of life here on Earth. I had been judging these parts in other people. Why can't people look at themselves? Why can't they do the work? Why do they project and numb and run and hide?

Yet how could I judge this in others when I had been one and the same? I had run. I had hidden. Judgement of others equals judgement of self. We all in our humanness simply do the best with the resources and knowledge we have at the time. For example, sometimes hiding behind a physical symptom is the best we can do. Sometimes this cycle will take years or even lifetimes to break. And how can we judge these patterns of distraction or avoidance in others, when at some point many of us have enacted the exact same behaviour?

And sometimes, this behaviour is the very thing we need to get through a moment of darkness. The gap, the pause, the rest, before we can pick ourselves up and proceed in connecting with what is yearning to be heard from our soul within.

Making Peace with Being a Human

Making peace with being a human, for me, was making peace with life. Making peace with the fact that I could probably never figure it all out, despite how much my mind wanted to. Making peace with the fact that it would never all be healed – and what would that mean anyway? Making peace with myself, not for what I had done, or achieved, or become in my life, but just for being me. Or rather for being me. For being the messy, complex, human soul who I was here on this Earth, for this very fleeting period of time.

For me, making peace with being a human, was freeing myself to actually live my life. To witness the beauty right in front of my eyes. To enjoy the embrace of my beloved. To wholeheartedly experience the connection with likeminded souls. To embody who I was born to be, in the physical form I was blessed to inhabit.

My time was Now.
Finally here.
Finally present.
Finally free.

For a moment. Then back to being a human.

Human. Soul. Human. Soul.

Separation. Wholeness. Disconnection. Unity.

One of the hardest things to make peace with as a human being, which some people face more intensely than others, is the loneliness we can feel deep within our core. Sometimes people believe that being in an intimate relationship will remove this feeling, and often it can be a reason why people chase them. Yet what I have found is that even being in a beautiful, loving relationship, doesn't remove this deep human feeling. Yet it is something so important to feel. To make peace with the loneliness of being a human, and to allow it to move through us when it arises. Without judgement. Without resistance. With pure, spacious awareness.

For when we take action driven from this place, the outcome can be negatively impacted by the intention to do something to fill a gap. When we strive for relationships, friendships or even jobs from a desire to remove this feeling, the energy of neediness has one of two outcomes. Either it brings in other needy energies, which is fraught with its own problems. Or it can drive further away from us, the very things that we yearn for. Connectedness, unity, oneness, and not to feel so alone.

When we can make peace with these feelings – that we were born alone, live our life in a world within us alone, and will die alone – and accept that as the human condition that it is, we can cultivate feelings of peace and acceptance. From this place, we can seek to find connection and oneness from within our very own soul. When we can find what we are searching for in the outside world inside of us, it shifts our energy. Then we can attract the relationships, friendships, jobs or circumstances, that will only fill us with more of this feeling.

We cannot find in the outside world something we have not yet found within ourselves. And so our job, when we want something in the outside world, is to cultivate it from within.

However, this is a process that takes time. We don't find connectedness, wholeness and oneness within overnight. Life is not meant to be a test, and whilst it is helpful to learn to find what we are looking for in the outside world within our own heart, it doesn't negate the benefits of taking positive action in the external world. As long as we have the awareness of these feelings and ensure we are not being driven by them, we can simultaneously take steps towards what we are seeking externally, whilst increasingly cultivating these feelings from within.

And why do we feel this deep disconnection and separation anyway?

Well, we are each half human, half soul. To say we are a spirit in human form, misses the point of human existence.

We are here, at this time, in this form, for a reason.

Yet before we incarnated here we were completely connected, existing in non-duality. That is, wholeness, interconnectedness, unity with all. Energy, spirit, one.

So when we are born into human form, we are born into duality. I and you. Separate selves. And this is what we resist, as we came from a oneness, a wholeness and a unity, only to face a void, an emptiness, a sense of disconnection.

The more we can find this sense of wholeness and connection within ourselves as humans, the more we can connect to the essence of who we really are as a soul.

It is the integration and meeting point of these two seeming polarities, that will bring us the feeling of connection we yearn for.

Restless soul.

Searching for what, I don't even know.

Cannot be found in a person, place, job or vocation.

Restless soul, restless soul. What are you searching for?

There is a yearning for something I can't quite put into words.

A place far from here.

A home.

A sense of connection.

An understanding.

Unity of soul and spirit. Merging of personality and essence.

Disconnected. Yet whole.

Fragmented. Yet together.

Will I ever find that which I am looking for?

Unknown, unknown.

So deeply unknown.

Pearls of Wisdom:

- Life is filled with polarities, and our journey is the integration of these aspects within ourselves.
- Ultimately, no one knows us better than ourselves. However, sometimes we need someone or something outside of ourselves, to help us access the inner wisdom we carry.
- Sometimes we will find the answers, and other times we will have to sit with the uncertainty of the unknown.
- To find what we are looking for in the outside world, we need to be cultivating it increasingly from within. Yet learning to be gentle and kind with ourselves as we move through this process, is also part of the journey.
- When we access the integration of our human and soul selves – when we find the meeting point between the two, and bring our soul into life through our physical form – we find the depth of connection we have always been seeking.

Wisdom Within:

1. What do I judge in others? Could this be something I am judging in myself?

2. Do I feel a sense of loneliness or separateness from others? When do I feel these feelings the most? What triggers these feelings to arise?

3. How can I cultivate a sense of connection from within? What makes me feel connected to myself, to life, to the interconnectedness of all things?

4. Is there anything I would like to bring into my external world, to create increased feelings of connection to myself, to others and to life?

Four

Following the Stepping Stones

I have found that life is a journey of following the stepping stones. One thing leads to the next, which leads to the next, and so on and so forth. When it came to healing the things that plagued me – physically, mentally, emotionally and spiritually – there wasn't really one moment when everything just clicked into place, like I thought there would be. It was a series of moments, connected by a thread of divine guidance by the Universe.

I learnt invaluable lessons with each practitioner I saw along the way. Each naturopath, body talk practitioner, shaman, hypnotherapist and acupuncturist helped me peel back yet another layer of the onion, that is the journey of true healing. Getting to the root cause of an issue is not a simple feat, as often there are many factors at play.

This uncovering journey, which is more like a shedding process, requires much patience, much trust, and above all, faith that things are working out exactly as they should be. Faith in the orchestration of life. Faith in the Universe's plans for us on our life path, and in the soul contracts that we agreed to embark upon in this lifetime.

Thus, the journey in itself provides the most invaluable lessons. Becoming a patient person, for example, is not something that comes naturally to many of us as human beings. When we want something, we want it now!

Having an unwavering faith in the bigger picture of our lives, when in discomfort or in pain – this too is not an easy feat. Thus the journey of healing provides layer upon layer of learning. Not only are we uncovering the things in our psyche, in our soul, that yearn to be healed and resolved, but we are also uncovering our personality's responses to adversity, our resilience, our strength, and our courage to face the darkness and transmute it into light.

And above all, we must discover the value of self-compassion. Of learning to treat ourselves with the utmost care and nurturing, as we embark on this journey. Recognising the magnificence that lies within us in being willing to face the truth, rather than covering it up with the distractions and pleasures of human life.

That being said, for those of us who tend towards the esoteric and skies above, we must remember the value and importance of our grounded human life. The integration of our two worlds. That the spiritual is to be found within the material.

When we connect with our humanness, we can find our joy in the ordinary. Letting the ordinary become extraordinary. This gives us the sustenance and fuel we need to withstand the demands of our spiritual life. Of the things spirit is asking us to transcend and transmute.

It is within our human lives that we find the diamond moments to sustain us. Laughing with a loved one. Snuggling on the couch with our beloved. Connecting with a dear friend and finding joy in the magic of just being in one another's company. It is in these moments that we are shown just how magical human life can be.

As we uncover the layers of conditioning and ego within us that are not the true essence of who we really are, the more we can let them go, or be, to discover the greater freedom of living awareness.

And it is this that is the true purpose of life. Not to find the perfect career, partner or house. Not to live the life we think we should live, but to shed the layers of ourselves that are not us, to embody more and more fully the essence of our soul. Our true nature. To find the extraordinary in the ordinary. To be grateful for simply being alive. To be honest and truthful, even if it may hurt another – not intentionally to do so, but to create an honest world. We cannot be truly loving and kind if we are withholding our truth. If we are saying just what we think someone wants us to say. Truth equals freedom. Will you set yourself free?

Pearls of Wisdom:

- Speaking our truth is the key to liberation.
- Healing is a series of moments that move toward a higher state of physical, mental, emotional and spiritual health.
- The journey itself is the greatest teacher. It is through the process of healing that we learn the lessons we were always meant to learn, if we open up to the messages our body, mind and soul are trying to tell us.
- Self-compassion is paramount. There is no true compassion for others, until we can first learn to be compassionate with ourselves.
- The integration of our spiritual and human selves, is the way towards living a soul embodied human life.

Wisdom Within:

- Do I feel free to speak my truth? Where or with whom can I speak my truth more freely?

- What are some of the current lessons that my life journey is calling me to learn? Can I embrace these lessons instead of resisting the process?

- Am I compassionate with myself? How can I bring in more self-compassion?

- Do I feel more connected to my human or spiritual self? How can I cultivate greater integration of these two aspects of my being? How can I live a more soul-embodied human life?

Five

Yearning to Surrender

For most of my life I have felt a yearning in my heart and soul for something that I don't think even exists yet. What is this call? I honestly am not sure, but on a deeper level I feel it is connected to the call to write. To express what is in my heart, even if simply for the act of expression. For no goal, objective or purpose, but simply for the joy in doing so.

So many of us move about our lives striving, pushing, and trying to make everything happen. We have bought into the collective consciousness that "good things take hard work". But I challenge you to question whether this is truly so.

When an artist paints and is in flow, when a dancer dances allowing their soul to move their body, when I sit at my laptop and my fingers move without my seeming control, are these things really hard work?

When we unite our soul with our human personality, we can experience a merging of the divine and human form. This requires us to discover what it really is that makes our soul come alive. When we find what this is, or the things in which we enter into the flow state, we discover what could be linked to our unique human missions here on this Earth.

And this is something that is always changing, always in evolution, always in flux. The less pressure we put on ourselves to find that one soul purpose, which is only limiting our vast potential, the more we are able to flow with the multitude of purposes we were sent here to fulfil. Whether they are linked to our career or vocation, or parenting a child, or volunteer work, or sharing our unique message with the world through a creative pursuit, each soul purpose has a certain quality to it. It feels as if we were always meant to do this particular thing, or be in this particular role, and that the Universe was always conspiring to draw us back to these missions.

When we let go our ego's grasp on our lives – which seeks order, control and what is known – we can settle into the uncertainty that underpins every human life. No one knows how their life will unfold. When we can truly sit with this, instead of letting it propel us into fear, we can transmute the fears into excitement, curiosity and wonder, about where it could all end up.

Nature reflects to us the magnificence and power of surrender. When I look out at the ocean, the vastness, the depth, the endlessness … it reminds me of the infiniteness and expansiveness of the human soul.

We are all so endless. So timeless and so magnificent. Yet so many of us cannot see this divine beauty within us.

We are so conditioned to be critical – to judge, to condemn, and to scrutinise every essence of who we are. All without realising that these external identifications are not the truth of our being.

We are divine and perfect exactly as we are, if only we could see it. If we could just let go, and surrender to the flow of life.

To whatever it is, that is meant for us.

For what is working its way into our consciousness, our life path, and our journey in each moment.

When we get quiet enough to really listen – to deflect the distractions from the ever-changing, ever-loud and intrusive external world – we can hear how our soul, our truth, our higher self, is communicating to us in every minute here on Earth. We are all being guided. When we connect with the voice of knowing within, and then have the courage to listen, we can cultivate the strength to act on what we hear and take the steps forward in the direction of our life's true path.

And this is where the magic lies. This is where we experience pure joy, the ecstasy of life as it is unfolding right here, right now, in this one moment. The beauty of the night sky, the crashing of waves against the shore, the glances between lovers, the bud of a new flower … there is ecstasy and bliss all around us, if we simply open our eyes to the magic.

But we need to let go of the fear-based collective consciousness of our modern world. We need to see through the illusions that are all around us.

Money. External power. Materialism. Self-sacrifice. Martyrdom. Surrendering our power into the hands of others. Doing the "right thing" out of fear rather than love. Compromising our dreams, our needs, our yearnings, for the sake of keeping the peace and staying within the margins of life as we know it.

Allowing our fears of the unknown and of change to keep us stuck, preventing us from expansion into the fullest and most wondrous version of who we are capable of being.

Letting life pass us by, without communicating to the world the secrets and gifts unique to our personality, our human self in this incarnation, here on Earth.

What a tragedy this would be to die with our magic still within us, never having been expressed and shared with the world.

So what can we do to tune in to ourselves, when so many of us are racing around at such a rapid pace through life, that there is little room to face what lies within the chambers of our magnificent hearts? And do we really even want to listen, if this meant letting go of everything as we knew it? Of life as we knew it. Of every belief, opinion, thought and idea we had of life, ourselves and the world in which we exist?

So many shy away from the Path, because from our ego position, our fear-based smaller self, this is just too scary. Too overwhelming. Too unknown. We get tricked into believing that we are better off leaving things as they are, because life is safer that way. We know what to expect. Or so we think.

Life has a way of redirecting us to where we need to be, for the full expansion of our soul's growth.

When we choose not to pay attention to the cues that are constantly infiltrating our consciousness, we can develop dis-ease in our bodies, or experience some other significant life event or circumstance. Although at first we may resent these apparent inconvenient occurrences, in actual fact they often arise to shake us out of our illusory lives. The lives we have worked so wilfully to create in an attempt to keep ourselves safe, and instead propel us into a life truly aligned with our soul.

My journey shifted me on a completely different trajectory in exactly this way. For many years I had been wilfully pushing at life, forcing myself along in the direction my small egoic self led me to believe was what I wanted. I was asleep and unaware of the reality and truth, the truthful path that my soul yearned to embark upon. Yet what I also came to realise, was that ultimately this truthful path is never in fact fixed – and in reality there is no Universal truth. Things are always changing, life is always in flux. What I desire and believe today – about life, about myself, about what I think I like, or need, or yearn for – changes tomorrow. Or if not tomorrow, then next week, next month, or even next year. And if this is so, what can we actually rely on? Where do we find a sense of stability, certainty or security, in this completely unpredictable, uncertain world?

The only answer I discovered – the only constant, unchanging, secure foundation that I could always trust in, to keep me going through the highs and lows of life – was that Divine essence within my heart and soul. That part of myself, just like that part in all of us, that is there from the moment we are delivered into this world, until the moment we take our very last breath. That part of me that bears witness to it all. That part of me that connects with the Divine, the Divine in you, the Divine in the world, the Universe, and all that cannot be comprehended or known by our human brains and consciousness. That centre, that wholeness that exists deep within. That can never be lost, as it is the essence of what we truly are. Love. The very core of our essence is Divine Love. Pure. Open. Trusting and safe.

What I discovered as I embarked upon the tumultuous journey within – a path not for the fainthearted – was my heart's ability to cultivate a depth of love and compassion for all beings. I uncovered this unconditional love and awe for all life is, through opening to it all. Through allowing myself to feel the depths of each positive and negative state capable to my being. Through knowing the depths, the lows of where our emotions can take us – the pain, the heartbreak, the loneliness, uncertainty, fear, despair, sadness, and everything that we instinctively run from out of our biological wiring to avoid pain. Through sitting with it all, feeling it, letting it engulf the entirety of my being, and coming to realise that I could still survive, I could still endure. This is how I came to know its opposite.

I am not saying that this is the only way. How could I know anyway? My way is not your way. Despite our interconnectedness and essence being one and the same, we are all paradoxically so different.

Yet I have found that it is through the process of surrendering – which is not a once off action, but rather an ongoing intentional state of being of deeply accepting rather than resisting whatever arises within the context of our life situation – we can discover the deepest of love for life. For ourselves. For our fellow human beings. For the effort and grace with which we all walk this Earth, doing the best we can, given each of our particular life circumstances. No one has it easier or harder than another – this too is an illusion. Whichever road we choose to take, life presents its challenges and obstacles for us all. We are all united in our humanness. And yet to find freedom, ultimately the journey is to discover who we really are. That Divine essence. That eternal self. That part of us that is connected to all that is.

Do you choose to be free?

Yearning to Surrender

Flow.

Grasping to the old. Attach.

Follow the call.

Time to move on.

We want the safety of the known. The good experiences of the past.

We cling and hold with all our might.

Don't let go.

Hold.

However, in doing so we fill our space with memories.

Not enough room left for the new.

Living in the past.

Even if we went back to that place, those circumstances and events, we could never recreate something that has already been.

We can lose our capacity for growth.

Stagnate.

So what is the alternative?

Allow.

Surrender.

Let life pass through us.

Move with where we are being guided.

Without resistance.

Feel the grief.

The sadness of letting go of things past.

And at the same time, allow the excitement of new experiences to fill our being.

The unknown can be a magical, exciting adventure, if we choose to create the space for it to enter into our experience.

What will you choose?

Attach or allow?

Resist or flow?

Let go.

Let go.

Yearning to Surrender

Pearls of Wisdom:

- When we connect our soul with our human personality, we can uncover the unique missions for our lives.
- Hard work is the illusion we buy into. We can choose to buy into a new belief, that right work, is body infused by soul.
- When we find what makes us come alive, we are filled with an energy, a momentum, a guiding force that lets our soul speak through the form of our physical body.
- We have multiple soul missions in this lifetime, and when we can take the pressure off finding just one, we expand our unlimited potential.
- Making peace with uncertainty, is the key to uncovering the freedom to discover the magic in our lives.
- Surrendering to the flow of where our life is taking us, is far easier than wilfully pushing our way through our lives.

Wisdom Within:

- What makes my soul light up? When do I feel in flow, in joy, energised and alive?

- What do I feel is my current soul mission? Where is my spirit guiding me to direct my attention right now? What is the Universe calling me to do or transcend?

- How do I feel about the uncertainty of life? How can I make peace with the future being so out of my control? Where in my life can I let go of holding the reins so tightly?

- Do I feel surrendered to the flow of where my life is taking me? Can I surrender even more?

Six

Trusting the Intuitive Voice Within

My medical journey began in Year Ten, when I wrote a letter to my future self stating "I want to be a doctor." In my adolescent naivety, how could I know how this choice would unfold into the twenty year struggle that it did? Medicine was one of my greatest teachers in learning to wholeheartedly trust my inner voice.

From my very early days as a medical student, once I reached hospital and clinic placements, the doubts about my suitability for this career path began. I felt I could never learn all the knowledge required, as the main way of teaching medical students in the clinical years was through putting us on the spot, asking us questions in front of our peers. This made me very anxious and put me into a freeze state, from which I just wanted to escape. And so I did. I spent as little time as I possibly could at the hospitals and somehow managed to get through the degree. However, even when I finished medical school I felt that I couldn't possibly have retained all of the knowledge required to work as a doctor, as I had been so anxious throughout it.

As a junior doctor, probably in my intern year, I remember crying to my mother from the toilet cubicle in the hospital during a panic attack state. The intensity of the responsibility and knowledge required was just so overwhelming. My intern year was a series of anxiety-provoking situations – from dealing with psychiatric patients and the host of physical issues that they presented with, with little support from the psychiatric doctors, to after-hours shifts being on call for multiple hospital wards, to acute presentations in the Emergency Department – making me one stressed out junior doctor!

I remember trying to get some help with managing the intense anxiety I felt, specifically related to the on-call shifts. I went to my "mentor" who happened to sit on the Medical Board. But instead of supporting me through this, he threatened that should I not complete my required after-hours work I would not pass my intern year, with very little interest in my mental health and wellbeing. I felt so trapped. I had studied six years at university to get to this point. So I decided that if I could just get through the intern year, everything would be okay.

I already talked about leaving medicine, maybe becoming a teacher. But this just didn't seem realistic, and so I persisted. During this first year as a qualified doctor I knew I had to get out of general medicine, and so straight away I applied to a speciality training program in psychiatry.

This proved to be filled with many new challenges that I could never have anticipated. Having to deal with drug-induced psychotic patients, suicidal patients, severely depressed patients requiring electroconvulsive therapy – amidst the myriad of other traumatic circumstances that I encountered on those wards – was certainly not something I had been prepared for. After three years I was completely burnt out, depressed myself, and at the same question mark point in my career. What should I do?

I decided to leave the psychiatry training program, the cost to my own mental health was just far too great. I had no idea what I would do, and the depression that I fell into took many months to transcend.

During that time I enrolled in a Certificate of Counselling, as I'd always had an interest in helping others and in mental health, given the experiences in my life thus far. I also embarked on two years of gestalt psychotherapy training, which was an eye-opening experience in itself. The process of learning was through observing participants in the group have a therapy session with the trainer. This I found incredibly overwhelming, as being an empath and highly sensitive person, the intensity of the energy in these sessions was far too great for me to manage.

Through both programs I gained some invaluable knowledge though, and proceeded on my journey, attempting to set up a private counselling practice. However, I found it difficult to build up a client base, as even I was unclear as to what I was actually offering. Was I a doctor, or a counsellor? And if I was a counsellor, did I really have all the tools I needed to practice in this role? I was not a psychologist, and so the doubts and insecurities about my ability to work in this capacity ran high, despite my psychiatry training, innate emotional intelligence, and being supported and encouraged by my psychology colleagues to do so.

This corresponded with the falling apart of my first marriage. Once the separation was official and I had moved out of the (his) house, I knew I needed to find a way to financially support myself. Even though I could have stayed in that relationship to ensure I didn't have to face financial uncertainty, I knew that I could not make this decision with the negative implication it would have on the lives of two souls.

So running back to medicine I went. I resumed working as a psychiatry doctor, as the income was lucrative and I needed a quick way to make some money. But deep within, I knew that I could not sustain this role. And so I embarked on the path of GP training.

In order to be eligible to begin the training, I had to up-skill in general medicine, as all I had really done after medical school was psychiatry. This was a monumental undertaking, as the only feasible option was "doing time" in addiction medicine and returning to the emergency department. Both were highly challenging in different, yet similar ways. The negative energy within the walls of the drug detox unit was all-encompassing, very similar to that which I had previously encountered within the psychiatric wards. I remember doing ward rounds and walking through the small unit barely able to drag myself around it, feeling as if I was walking through mud. The density and heaviness of the energy there was overwhelmingly suppressive, especially to my sensitive empath nature.

During my time there I also encountered some very wounded patients, which unfortunately had a significant negative impact on me as the un-empowered, un-energetically boundaried empath I was at that time. Sponging others' emotions, thoughts and feelings, was not something I wanted to be doing anywhere, never mind in this setting.

The emergency department was very different externally – fast-paced, heightened and always on high alert – yet had a similarly negative impact on me. The energy felt heavy and dense in my physical body, only magnified by the time I was required to be there, as the only option was to do ten hour shifts. I remember getting to lunch time and finally having the opportunity to sit down, but then honestly thinking that I didn't know how I was going to get up and make it through to the end of the shift.

At that stage, I wasn't yet aware about the concept of being a physical empath. I think I must have had some awareness of being an emotional empath though, absorbing others' emotions and feeling them as if they were my own, but I attributed the physical sensations to being a highly sensitive person in an overstimulating environment.

On reflection though, I have always been a physical empath. Different places or being around certain personalities significantly affects both my energetic and physical energy bodies. The difference between the two is that say you are in a place with a "bad vibe", you may feel this on an energetic level, but when that feeling turns into a physical sensation, like a heaviness in the body or fuzziness in the head, it has entered the physical body.

It can also sometimes be an intuitive sign that the place, person or situation is not a good match for you. Alternatively, it can reflect something that you may be picking up from within the person you are with – for example, an inconsistency between what is being externally portrayed and what may be happening within for that person – or from the environment in which you find yourself.

When we are somewhere aligned, or with someone who is good for us, our energy body can come alive. As a physical empath, this can be felt in the physical body as a surge of energy. It is a great feeling to be in the presence of someone who literally lights us up!

What I have subsequently discovered though, is that often when we are attuned to something in others, we similarly carry it within ourselves. So the key is not to bubble wrap ourselves from the outside world, as this would only shrink our lives, but to do our own emotional work. In doing so, we cultivate self-responsibility as we seek to clear the layers of our own emotional "baggage", making us less sensitive to detecting and resonating with it in others.

The relationship with medicine that I had over all those years, is a good example of how we can delay listening to our intuitive voice within. This may be due to the fears that we carry in our minds, as well as the pressures we may absorb from the external world. I kept pushing myself along a track that was not simply challenging in a good, inspiring and productive way, but instead was draining, demoralising, and detrimental to my being on all levels. I would come home from the emergency shifts, eat something, and then lie down on the couch in a state of oblivion, completely energetically depleted, before dragging myself off to bed. All the while, I kept thinking that if I just got to the GP setting, things would be so much better. Little did I know.

The GP setting was fraught with many of its own challenges. The expectations in a traditional GP clinic are to see on average at least four patients every hour. Even to an empowered empath this would be a significant undertaking! Here I learnt some important lessons about boundaries, human behaviour, and learning to be true to yourself.

I tried very hard to summon positive energy as I started each new day in GP practice, saying mantras on my way to work, attempting to manifest like-minded patients and find moments of joy whilst there. Yet like Groundhog Day, each shift I would be slammed with the pressures, expectations and demands of patients who had been trained by the medical system to absolve any sense of responsibility for their own health, and place it wholly in the hands of the treating doctor.

Occasionally I would meet like-minded patients, who had a different energy about them. They held their "stuff". They were a pleasure and a joy to work with, and were like crumbs from the Universe reminding me why I was still in a healing profession. But these were in the minority. Deep down I knew I was not in the right role, as I had never felt like I could fully be myself. I felt enmeshed in a system that placed little value in the way that I wanted to help people. It felt inauthentic for me to perpetuate the idea to patients, that their body was a separate entity to what was going on in their mind, emotions and soul. I could no longer practice within a belief system that viewed symptoms as inconvenient random occurrences, whilst holding such a strong belief in the physical form being a reflection of deeper processes within the mental, emotional and spiritual levels.

At the same time I was still facing my own health challenges, with chronic symptoms that were severely affecting the quality of my everyday life. Even though intuitively I knew that this was related to how I felt in my job, I could not yet face the steps that I would need to take to address what my body was crying out for me to hear.

Finally though, the time came when I could push myself down this path no longer. My soul was now crying out for me to stop. I was deeply suffering, in my thoughts, my body and my heart. It was time. Time to listen to the intuitive hits that I had been getting all along. To summon the courage to embark on a different path. Not a clear, traditional path of apparent "security", which is really just an illusion as at any time our life circumstances can change. But the path of a pioneer. Of seeing something that others don't. The path of being creative and true to myself, and bringing everything I had learnt along the way into an integrated offering. My soul path. By trusting that intuitive voice within, I could finally be free.

Pearls of Wisdom:

- When we go against the voice of our intuition, we will suffer.
- There may be important lessons for us to learn, but wilfully pushing life in a direction not meant for us cannot end well.
- The body will reveal signs to us if we keep going against the inner voice within. Initially these may be subtle, like fatigue or low energy, but the more we push and the longer it goes on for, the louder the body will have to shout to get our attention, with chronic unexplained symptoms or illness.
- When we can get quiet enough to listen to the intuitive voice of our soul within, and take action from the guidance we hear, we begin the process of alignment with our true path.
- What is meant for us will flow, will unfold with a greater ease, and will be supported in unexpected ways by the Universe.
- It can be scary to act on the intuitive hits we receive, not knowing exactly how they will unfold, but what is scarier is living a life of suffering, due to the grip of fears that can keep us stuck.
- Finding ways to connect with our intuition, is the key to learning how to tune in. It is a journey of discovery to find what enables us to connect to that

Trusting the Intuitive Voice Within

still place inside of us, whether it be a place, activity or practice. Going around in circles on topics in our head, is a sure sign that the voice of the ego has taken over. Mind equals ego. Our job is to watch and witness this, but use it as a sign that there is something deeper our soul is trying to communicate with us.

Wisdom Within:

- When do I feel most connected with my intuition or higher-most self?

- Do I have any physical symptoms in the body? If so, could these be signs from within that I am not listening to my intuition?

- If I was talking to myself as the physical symptom in my body, or as the organ or body part causing me discomfort or pain, what would I be saying? For example: *Talia, this is your gut speaking. It is time to let go of …*

- Is there something my intuitive compass within is guiding me to do, but the fear of taking necessary action is getting in the way?

Seven

Being Honest with Yourself

All along, I knew I was running.

For over a decade, I spent my time in constant flight. Putting out the flames of the dramas in my life. Wishing I could be free of all these outside world challenges.

Subconsciously, there was something deeper at play.

The outside world was simply a creation by my inner subconscious landscape, trying to keep me safe from facing the things I was running from.

I knew I was running, but I didn't fully realise that I was running from myself. Or maybe I did. But still I chose not to stop. How could I face myself? My feelings. Those really uncomfortable, challenging, unpleasant emotional states – the ones we all instinctively run from.

Loneliness. Emptiness. Isolation. Loss of sense of self.

Due to the years I had spent working with people going through transitions in their lives – like divorce, moving house, retirement, or loss of a loved one – when I finally came face to face with what I had been running from, I knew I was not alone.

Helping me connect with the interconnectedness of us all as human beings. Providing an ironic sense of comfort in my aloneness.

I had finally decided, for the third time, to leave medicine in the traditional sense I had known it. The time had come to let go of the GP training program and embark on my own holistic version of health and healing. I knew I had the skills and I most certainly had the experience. But the space that was created by the decision to let something so big go, was so big! So vast and expansive. Leaving me feeling so completely lost.

This is what many of us face at transition points in our lives. Loss of identity. *Who am I?*

Many of us rationally know that we are not the roles we play, how can we be something that can be taken away from us? Yet when it goes, there is this hole, this deep, endless, empty void.

I knew it was the right thing to have done, every intuitive hit had taken me down this path. It was finally time to face the truth that I had been withholding from my conscious mind.

I had to be honest with myself.

That I had created the drama.

I had not been able to face the void. The emptiness within.

This came despite having the most beautiful, loving partner, as it is separate to being loved by an outside source. It is different to even loving yourself. It is a very deep and mostly concealed aspect within the human soul, that lives in a state of duality and separation. The realisation that in our human form, we are apart in the physical sense from all else.

Yet in this deepest confrontation with the duality of existence, I came to find the interconnectedness and non-duality of life. That on the level of our soul, we are all connected to the same divine essence.

At our core, within the deepest part of us, we find that when we can truly stop and feel the feelings we have been running from, they are given permission to emerge and move through us. We do not need to hold on to these states, and rather can allow them to surface and then evaporate into the Universe. And this process takes, as long as it takes. Sometimes, when we have been running from something for so long, the process of alchemising it – of allowing it to engulf us, to then move through us – can take a bit of time. And this is where we need to bring in a loving compassion for ourselves, as we face our shadow parts.

My experience of facing this separateness, meant facing the fact that in our human form, we are all fundamentally alone. Alone experiencing a world within us – beyond the constructs of job, marital status and parental role, amongst the myriad that we inhabit – we find the truth of who we really are, simply just essence, energy, matter. Paradoxically, anything but simple.

We discover that we no longer need to pull these roles so close to our skin, to cover up a feeling of not being enough as we are.

We are all valuable and significant just for being alive. Our existence and essence as life itself, is the miracle.

There is no accomplishment, worldly material possession, status, role, or outcome, that will ever come close to filling that connection we yearn for to the innermost state of our being.

Yet, when we can discover our soul as the miracle itself, we realise that the things we may have been chasing were illusory anyway.

It is this realisation that can liberate us. We can find our freedom. Then there comes the ability to make conscious choices in our lives, rather than living governed by a fear-based conditioned matrix of illusions.

From this place of vast emptiness, yet paradoxically extreme magnificence, we can then call in an external world that we truly wish to inhabit. An external world that is in alignment with the inner truth of who we actually are.

It can be a journey to cultivate a life that reflects who you are within, however this is just the process. The process

Being Honest with Yourself

allows the removal of everything that doesn't resonate and is not you, to allow the emergence of your true light to shine through.

When we let go our fears of facing the unknown, and surrender our control (or illusion of it), we can embark on the uncovering of that which is truly who we are.

When we can connect with this spark, this essence, and find ways of shining it through into the external world, this is where we find the magic and joy of life.

Pearls of Wisdom:

- Facing our aloneness, facing the things we run from, sitting in the emotions that we feel will consume us if we dare to feel them – this is the process of allowing the transmutation of darkness into light.
- We think that if we allow ourselves to feel the more painful human emotions, then we will get stuck in them, but ultimately nothing lasts forever.
- The more we allow ourselves to really feel our emotions, the quicker they can actually move through us, instead of getting pushed under the rug into the crevices of our body.
- The body will store the emotions we have not yet processed and set free, and this will manifest as physical symptoms if it goes on for too long.
- The paradox is that by confronting our duality, our separateness as a human being from everyone and everything else, we can connect with the interconnectedness of all things, and our non-duality with life.
- We are not the roles we play. So the more we can make peace with this, the less we will need the Universe to wake us up from the illusions we have bought into, by presenting us with some major life circumstance.

Being Honest with Yourself

Wisdom Within:

- When I spend time alone, what are some of the feeling states that commonly arise?

- Do I have any unhelpful behaviours that distract me from facing these feelings? This can include spending time with people or in situations that don't serve me, just to fill the time.

- Can I start to actually feel my emotions in order to allow them to move through me? How might I do this? Do I need to access any support in dealing with uncomfortable feelings?

- Do I overly identify with the roles I play within my life? How can I release my attachment to these roles?

Eight

When Enough's Enough

There came a point along my journey at which I finally stopped to realise, that the time had come to let go my addiction to seeking. For so long I had been chasing this concept of being healed, whether from issues of the mind, the body or the spirit. But it got to the point at which I couldn't remember not being in a period of seeking healing from someone outside of myself.

Through this awareness, I came to the realisation that the next part of my healing journey, was in actually living my life. Taking myself out of the victim role that I had played so incredibly well, and shifting into the role of an empowered person. I had been bypassing actually living my life with an endless search to heal every last trigger, every last negative thought, and every last symptom in my body. Simply allowing myself to live and be happy, had become such foreign concepts to me.

There is a fine line between tuning into and listening to the messages the body is trying to tell us, and keeping a symptom alive through our intense fixation and preoccupation with it. And the key lies in knowing the difference. Knowing when to tune in, and knowing when to tune out. Knowing when distraction is actually a good thing, when we learn how to distract ourselves with the right things. Connecting with others. Doing the things that we love and trying new things. Finding what brings us joy and makes us come alive.

We can arrive at these points along our journeys when, even for a moment, we have reached the end of our seeking. The end of seeking all the answers, outside intervention, or the missing piece that will somehow solve it all.

I started to realise that my ego had formed an attachment to the role of needing to be healed. I even had to consider that perhaps I was deriving some kind of secondary gain from holding myself back, with either physical symptoms or repetitive intrusive thoughts. Maybe I wanted to hold onto the energy and attention of a healing professional, maybe it was the fear of the emptiness that would come by letting go of the search, or maybe it was something else outside of my awareness. But intuitively I knew that the time had come. Enough's enough. Time to stop seeking. Time to find the resources I needed from within. No more new modalities. No more new professionals. I had myself and for now I needed to learn to live with that alone.

The ego is very sneaky though, and I started to notice that the more my life shifted in a positive direction in the outside world, the more my psyche created symptoms of the mind and the body to keep me stuck. And so I had to rewire my psyche, which had held onto the belief that I didn't deserve happiness and that happiness itself was unsafe, that I wholeheartedly deserved all the miracles and blessings of my life. And that I was in fact safe within my mind, and within my life.

And I realised that this part of the puzzle, this part of the healing, was in fact a choice. I could choose to keep calling in the voice of ego. Of fears, of paranoias, and of doubts. Or I could just move on. Notice the voice. Allow it. Hear it. Show compassion for it. Let it shout and scream and try its best to bring me down, and then let it get softer and less frequent as it burnt itself out. As I realised that I didn't need it anymore. I could get the love and attention it was seeking first and foremost from within, but also through just being myself, as the empowered, strong and courageous human being that I was.

I didn't need to create symptoms to get validation. I didn't need to create intrusive thoughts to feel safe. I could, and would, just move on. With the voices of doubt. With the fears. With the insecurities and the imperfections. It was time to shift the focus.

To bring in more light. To see that the battle I had been fighting had been an illusory one, as the problems weren't even real.

The time had come to set myself free …

And soon enough the time came to seek help, yet again.

This unfolded through the realisation that I had been bypassing my feelings, as a result of absorbing conditioned ideas from the spiritual collective. The pressure to always see the best in others, to always be happy, to always cultivate the higher way, came crashing heavily down.

The thoughts were getting louder.

The body stopped releasing, after five months of nearly daily bowel motions following a "miraculous" hypnotherapy session.

The emotions intensified.

And although on one hand I couldn't quite understand why this was all happening, on the other, I felt some kind of relief.

It wasn't only the stool that my body was holding in. It was the sadness. The anger. The frustration. The grief. But mostly, even after all the time that had passed, still the heartbreak.

In the past my heart had been shattered. Not in two, but into a million little pieces that I thought would never get put back together again. And all those years ago, I had made the decision to bubble wrap my heart. Lock it up and throw the key away, after the heartbreak that had been.

But the body doesn't care about time, space, physical reality. It just exists. And with enough time and sufficient inner work, I had finally let love in again. Opened my heart to the most beautiful, wonderful man. What had unfolded through allowing in this connection, was the creation of the most amazing, magical relationship. Feeling safe in his presence. Free to be myself. So loved, cared for and cherished.

And then came the trip for our wedding. I had been through this process before and had buried it deep within. But as a result of these unhealed wounds lying dormant within the chambers of my mind and heart, the fear of things not working out and of losing the one I loved, surfaced with a vengeance. I felt like I was in some kind of time warp, where I had brought all the anger, all the sadness, and all the fear from the past, into my present reality. That past relationship still haunted me.

My heart had not yet healed. I had nurturing and repairing still to do.

And although being with my beloved had opened me back up to love, it was now up to me to tend to old wounds. To find the resources within to overcome the traumas of the past.

It wasn't going to be easy to confront the feelings I had kept buried, but the only way to really allow my love's love in, was to move through the wounds of past hurts. Only by feeling what needs to be felt and letting it move through you, can it actually move through you – and not stay stuck like a stool in your gut that won't move the sh*t through!

Pearls of Wisdom:

- Knowing when to seek help and knowing when to stop the search is the key.
- We can get addicted to anything, even things that can be good for us. When we keep playing out a certain role, despite our desire to take a break or do something different, there may be a secondary gain our ego is receiving by playing out these patterns.
- The key lies in self-awareness, as only we know when we actually need help outside of ourselves or when we are being called to navigate life with our own devices.
- The healing search can be a way of bypassing life and not facing the feelings that we may not want to feel, like loneliness, emptiness or lack of validation. Spiritual practices and philosophies can also keep us stuck, if we buy into the notion that feeling happy is the only permissible feeling there is.
- When we can give ourselves the validation we need, and sit with any uncomfortable emotions that may arise without seeking outside salvation, we are moment by moment shifting from a victim role to an empowered state of being.
- However, there will always be times within each of our lives when we exhaust our inner resources to cope with the circumstances we are faced with. During these times when we are called to seek help

from outside of ourselves, we are called to do so with loving kindness and a compassionate attitude toward ourselves. Letting go of any self-judgement, and instead cultivating a wholehearted acceptance for wherever it is that we find ourselves to be.

When Enough's Enough

Wisdom Within:

- Is it time for me to seek outside support, or is it time to let it go and rely on my own devices?

- Is there a secondary gain I may be receiving by constantly seeking outside support?

- Do I seek to feel happy all of the time, or am I comfortable allowing all the emotions I experience to arise and then move through me?

- If I am really honest with myself, do I identify with being in a victim role right now? If so, what is my next right move to make the shift to an empowered state of being?

Nine

Light and Love and Being Unf*ckwithable

For a large portion of my life I subscribed to the spiritual idea of sending light and love to others, even to those who had done the wrong thing by you. However, there came a point at which I discovered just how much this way of operating did not serve me. It did, in fact, allow unfathomable circumstances to go on for far longer than they should have!

I had always been someone who saw the best in other people – even those whom had been institutionalised for aggression or violence, drug addiction, and psychotic or antisocial behaviour. In these circumstances it came very naturally to me, to hold in mind that behind their suffering and acting out, at their core was a soul that was inherently divine love. A lovely and perhaps true, but also naive outlook, that can only get you so far!

Through a situation in which I was called to deal with some very unpleasant neighbours though, I learnt that at some point you have to draw the line! People aren't their behaviours, but they are responsible for them. It is lovely to see the best in others, but it is self-detrimental to excuse toxic behaviour fired in your direction.

This series of encounters was the Universe's way of teaching me the invaluable lesson of boundaries. I had been so focussed on spreading light and love and helping others to heal, that it had come at the expense of my self, my peace, my safety and my sanity! And so the Universe had to clearly, albeit a little harshly, show me the value in not only being someone who spread light and love in the world, but also in becoming someone who was unf*ckwithable!

I was called to stand in my power, call toxicity out, and finally acknowledge that I was not responsible for facilitating the healing of everyone whom I met.

I think this is a lesson that many of us with empathic and sensitive natures have to learn. Boundaries. Letting go of taking an over-responsibility for others. Inner power. Self-respect. And to question why we believe we are so responsible for others anyway. What potential ego gain could be keeping us stuck in a saviour/rescuer role, that never serves us? And could we have become fixated on helping, healing and taking care of those outside of ourselves, due to perhaps being unable to direct this within?

We may even have to consider that at the root of our overly altruistic nature, there may lie a sense of unworthiness – due to our value attached to our capacity to heal, or of feeling undeserving of all the love and care we outpour to others. At these turning points in our lives we can come to realise that we have a choice to do things differently. To redirect some of that loving, compassionate energy within, towards our very own selves.

Light and love is wonderful, but sometimes we just need to tell someone or something to get f*cked! This might be more in a metaphorical sense though, as we won't be winning over many friends by going around saying such things. But rather in the energy we project. We have to stand up for ourselves. No lawyer, courtroom judge, family member or friend, can do the work we are being called to do. It can even be towards a thought process in our very own head. With OCD there comes a time at which you are so f*cking fed up with intrusive thoughts, that you decide to say, "F*CK OFF!"

And I think this is really what happened with me.

One day I came back from a walk. A simple walk and my body started having an episode of intractable gas. It sounds funny and almost ridiculous, but in that moment I honestly thought I could not go on. After half an hour of meditation and calming myself down, I realised that I had just had something of a panic attack, but manifesting through a symptom in the body! I had believed I was almost going to die and felt like I could not cope, feeling an intense sense of urgency and panic.

When I reflected honestly on what may have triggered this physical manifestation of likely an emotional reaction in my psyche, the only thing I could think of was the OCD thoughts that had still been haunting me. Round and round on repeat, like a f*cking record that won't shut up! It was then that I decided, "F*ck the OCD! I am done." And that was the beginning of seeing through the illusions of obsessive and ruminating thinking, and reclaiming my mind as my own. A similar lesson in developing boundaries in the outside world, but instead strengthening these boundaries within, against the incessant stream of an overactive ego.

Life is about paradox. We need to be kind and loving, and we need to be strong and assertive. We need to allow things to be felt, and to let go the resistance to emotions, physical symptoms and thoughts – and we need to tell them to f*ck off. There is no one fix, no one solution. Instead, we need to stay present to whatever is happening right now in the field of our conscious awareness, tune inwards, and work out our "next right move", as Oprah says, on how to proceed.

True healing is the discovery and embodiment of the understanding that there is nothing and no one out there that can save or rescue us. Sadly, as much as we might want it, that job is our own. But the liberation that comes from being able to go within, to self-soothe, and to find the answers that we seek from our very own soul, is true freedom.

Pearls of Wisdom:

- Light and love is wonderful, but sometimes life calls us to stand in our power and be unf*ckwithable!
- Boundaries in the external world and within our own minds are paramount.
- The body will manifest the mental, emotional, energetic and spiritual processes in our system, until we have learnt the lesson that the Universe is trying to teach us.
- We are our own saviour! It is up to each one of us to rescue ourselves.
- Our answers are not to be found in others or in the external world, as ultimately they will come from within.

*Light and Love and Being Unf*ckwithable*

Wisdom Within:

- Do I feel balanced between being overly assertive and overly passive in the world?

- In what area of my life or with whom might I need to strengthen my boundaries?

- Do I carry within any unhelpful thought processes or beliefs, or are there any behaviours that I engage in, which might require me to similarly strengthen my boundaries towards?

- Do I identify with projecting an energy of needing to be rescued? How might I become my own saviour?

Ten

Finding the Love of Your Life

So many people are on the search for love, for a life partner to share their journey with, as we have been conditioned to believe that this is the best way to live. I believe that it is so wonderful to share your life with someone, as it brings in a whole other dimension to life, for those who want this. Yet what I realised on my journey to manifesting a beautiful, loving partner in the external world, was that firstly, I needed to find the love of my life within.

The path to love, is really a path to love of self, as we cannot find outside of ourselves that which we have not yet found within. When I realised this, I embarked on a mission to cultivate a more loving relationship with myself. To addressing the barriers in my heart, that had been getting in the way of receiving the love I so desired from another.

Finding the Love of Your Life

And it was on this journey that what I came to realise on a heart level, was that I was love. I could be in a perpetual state of love – in love with myself, in love with life, in love with the magic and the beauty that was always around me in each and every moment, if only I opened my eyes to see it.

For so long, like so many of us, I was conditioned to believe that the only access to love – to those feelings of bliss, infatuation, ecstasy with life, pure joy and elation – was through the realm of an intimate relationship or an evolving potential connection with another. I believed that it was only through this type of interaction that we could access these feelings.

So for a time, I chased it. I ran from one new encounter to the next, in chase of that high, those feelings of bliss and ecstasy, that each new encounter activated in me.

The highs were incredible, blissful, magical. Taking my emotions to levels of such elation. Yet the lows and heartbreaks were so intense, so incredibly painful and deep. Disproportionate to the loss of the actual person who had triggered those feelings within me.

Time after time this would happen, until I came to the realisation that as a feeling person, I could connect with the feelings of love in a heartbeat. And it was not necessarily that the person in front of me was right for me, but rather that my own capacity for love was so great and so deep.

That as an empath and a sensitive soul I had so much love within my heart, that the moment someone came into my world with whom I developed a strong heart felt connection, I would access these deep feelings of love. And that these feelings were not coming from outside of myself – from any external person, circumstance or situation – but rather had been activated and triggered to rise to the surface of my being. Yet they were always my own feelings, from deep within my very own heart and soul.

And like so many foundational belief structures of our modern society, I came to see the search for love from any external source, for the illusion that it is. The true path to love is not in searching endlessly for another to love us and fulfil those needs within our soul, but to find that source of unconditional love from inside of ourselves. It is only once we have traversed the path through the terrains of our own being to access that love from within, that we have any hope of a real, deep, conscious and empowered type of love.

This realisation led to my understanding that it was my duty, one of my life's contracts, to work towards loving myself and loving life, more and more each and every day. And that it was only through embarking on this inner journey, that I would find the truest and purest of loves that I yearned for. Which then I did.

And then I wondered if maybe, just maybe this was the path for us all, when I considered how many humans here on Earth really, truly love and adore themselves. Not on an ego level – the level of form, physical appearance, job or financial status – but the true essence of who they really are.

How many of us were walking around in relationships that were dysfunctional, co-dependent, or even (on a less severe scale) holding us back from discovering who we really were? How many of us were settling, because we had bought into the conditioned belief that said we were only loveable, only worthy of love, if that love was coming from an outside source? Instead of being taught to see that we were always loved, loved by the greater source of all that is, just for being alive. Just for being our imperfect human selves.

That we could access love in each and every moment, when we could finally let go of the pressures, demands, expectations and illusions, we let run and dictate our lives. Allowing us to increasingly connect with the sense of beauty and love within us. In witnessing the dawn of a new day, the evening sunset, the stars at night, a new flower bloom. In holding a cup of hot tea in our hands on a cold day, being held by the comfort of our favourite chair – the possibilities were endless.

One day, I finally realised that I was love. I was the love I had always been searching for. I was such a loving, kind and beautiful soul, and it is this part of me that is the same as that part in you. That divine essence that is within each and every one of us.

We are all a fragment of the divine Universal Love.

The entirety of the Universe always has, and always will, reside within each and every one of our very own hearts.

If we choose to see it.

And in that moment she realised how blessed her life really was …

She had everything she had ever truly desired … what her soul had truly desired, rather than the illusory wants the veil of her egoic conditioned smaller self, led her to believe she needed to be content and happy.

She had gained her freedom.

The freedom of awareness … that she was so much more than the limited thoughts her conditioned human brain created, more than the myriad of emotions she bared witness to each day.

She was more than the labels, titles and roles she played.

She was infinite and vast, deep and magnificent.

She was safe. She was secure. She had laid down her roots.

She now took such care of her beautiful self and no longer tolerated being treated with such disrespect.

She knew who she was. And that was where her power lay.

Finding the Love of Your Life

She could see through illusions. She had finally learnt that the word she heard and the word that was truly meant by the other, were not always one and the same.

Her delicious naivety and innocence had been shattered, but in a way that allowed her to become stronger and wiser.

Discernment was now her founding mantra. She would not just absorb everything from the outside world into her being, attempting to heal it all.

She would choose what was positive and uplifting to her spirit, her higher self. What aligned with the vibrational energy of her innermost being.

She was called.

And she responded with grace and devotion.

With radical acceptance, she followed the path of the Universe's call.

Pearls of Wisdom:

- The love of your life is you!
- To find something in the outside world, we need to be taking steps to cultivate it increasingly from within.
- When we look outside of ourselves to find something that we feel we lack, we can create relationships based on need rather than want. This sets up a dynamic of co-dependence, rather than the coming together of two interdependent people who have chosen to share their lives together.
- The realisation that love is a feeling cultivated from within your own heart, regardless of who stands before you, is a way of connecting to the source of unconditional love that lies deep within every one of us. That we have access to these feelings irrespective of whether we are currently in a romantic relationship or not. And that the more we tap into these feelings from within, the more likely we are to manifest an external love relationship into physical form.

Wisdom Within:

- What is my relationship with myself like?

- How can I strengthen my relationship with myself?

- How can I connect with the feelings of love, regardless of whether I am in a relationship or not?

- If I am in a relationship currently, when I closely examine it, do I think it is an interdependent or co-dependent dynamic? If it appears to be co-dependent, is this the right relationship for me? And if it is, how can I shift this relationship into a more interdependent dynamic?

Eleven

The Greatest Opponent You Will Ever Face

On my journey, I have discovered that the greatest obstacle to a human being's happiness, is the ego within. We often think that it is the circumstances of our lives that dictate how we feel, but in fact the opposite is true. Rather, it is our feelings and state of mind which are responsible for the creation of the world we see in front of our eyes.

Time and time again, I would experience a flare up of symptoms, be they of the body or mind. As a human being, my instinctive reaction was often something along the lines of, "How can I fix this? What new practitioner can I see? What new supplement can I take? What old story can I dig up to link to this symptom?" These are just some of the ways the mind, or ego, can distract us from what is truly at play.

And yes, sometimes we do need to see a new practitioner, take a new supplement, or heal a past wound. However, after a prolonged journey of "healing", I've found that there comes a point at which we have seen multiple practitioners, taken endless supplements, herbs and pills, endlessly explored our past to heal what needed to be healed … and still we can be faced with old symptoms that seem to be stuck in the body. What now?

This is when we have to go very deep within, and consider whether we may in fact be amidst an ego battle. Have we overcome so much, come so far, transmuted the darkest of dark into light, and are still somehow keeping ourselves stuck? Perhaps living in a state of "healing" for so long is a tricky role to unhook from? Perhaps the ego gains a sense of self through the role of needing to heal? Perhaps, despite our firm belief otherwise, we may be receiving some kind of secondary gain from the symptoms we face, be it attention, validation, or someone else's energy?

Allowing ourselves to actually be happy, to move on, and to be free, can be scary to the ego within us. This can often be an unfamiliar state, if we have traversed a landscape of darkness within. Although happiness appears to be filled with unlimited potential, in some way the human ego prefers to stay with what it knows, even if that place can be a place of suffering.

What is unknown can seem so out of control, which is what the ego is trying to protect us from. But ultimately, life is out of our control. Whether we choose to stay stuck or to let go and step into the unknown, we cannot predict the way in which our life will unfold. However, the potential of what we can experience when we let go the victim story of who we once were, is unlimited. And it is from this place that our soul can finally be free to live our life, at this time, in this current moment, unburdened by our story of the past.

EGO.

The voice of doubt.

The voice of fear.

Desperately clinging to a known and predictable way of being.

Time to release.

To let go its grip.

Surrender to the unfolding.

Unlimited and free.

So how do we overcome these ego battles, that no one else but ourselves could possibly even know that we are entering? Well, this is when the Universe is truly

The Greatest Opponent You Will Ever Face

summoning us to be fearless. To stop the search for our solutions in the outside world, and instead seek to find the resources we require for our battle, from within.

The key is in staying calm, connecting even more deeply with the witness observer part of ourselves, as we see whatever is to play out across the landscape of our body or mind. And to just notice the energy of it. Eventually the ego, in whatever form it presents, has a way of burning itself out. It eventually gets tired of the fight, and gives up, or at least gets quieter. And if we let go of the rope in the tug of war that we have been engaged in, and see that the part of us creating the symptoms and the part of us wanting them gone are actually one and the same, then the space arises from which we can discover our true nature. Our divine consciousness, that bears witness to it all. The constant, soft, gentle part of us that has been there since we were born, and will remain until the moment we take our very last breath.

Witness.
Watcher.
Conscious awareness.
And it is here, that we find our healing.
It is here that we become, finally free.

Pearls of Wisdom:

- The greatest battle we will ever face is the one within.
- Learning how to notice all the ways the ego can sneak in, is the key to stepping beyond it into the state of conscious awareness.
- Making space for the ego, accepting it rather than fighting or resisting it – even when it is seemingly causing havoc in our system – is the key to loosening its grip.
- We are so much more than the thoughts in our mind. Than the symptoms in our body. Than the emotions in our heart. We are the divine consciousness, that bears witness to it all.

The Greatest Opponent You Will Ever Face

Wisdom Within:

- When or with whom does my ego (fears/doubts/insecurities) get triggered most often in my life?

- Is my ego showing up through my thinking, feelings, behaviours, or physical symptoms in my body?

- How can I become more aware of when I am in the grip of an ego battle?

- Am I currently practicing meditation? What meditation practice helps me strengthen the conscious observer part of me within? Do I have something else that works better for me, to similarly connect with this deeper part of myself?

Twelve

Writing Your Own Story

1. Accept yourself.
   Your whole self. Not only the parts that you like or that others give you credit for. Accept your emotions. Your mind. Your body. Your uniqueness. Your quirks. Your apparent flaws. Your apparent imperfections. Embrace who you are at your core.

2. Be authentic in thought, word and action.
   Let go of trying to say what others expect you to say. Doing what is expected you will do with your life. Living as if you are trapped within the confines of a limited version of who you were truly meant to be. Spread your wings. Speak your truth. Dare to think

outside the confines of a conditioned world. Let go of what other people would think if they knew the real you. What you really stood for. What really lights you up. Just do that. Be that. Be who you were always meant to be.

3. Let go of what is not meant for you.
   People, circumstances, places. Have the courage to let life flow through you without holding on too tight. Allow the natural movement of what resonates with your current vibration, to move in, and gently out of your life. And always remember, that what is meant for you, will never pass you by.

4. Trust in your soul's purpose(s).
   Know that you were meant to be here, at this time, in this way, for a reason. Know that there are no coincidences to your existence, or any step along your journey. Everything is unfolding in a way of greatest benefit to your soul path and the evolution of the collective. Each day, strive to connect more deeply with the inner yearnings of your soul. Be guided by what and who makes you feel you can simply be yourself. Let the stepping stones of life guide you, along the journey meant for you.

5. Choose surrender over trying so hard.
   Let go of forcing and willing things to happen, and simply allow. Let your actions be fuelled by an energy of gentleness, ease and grace. Know that we are all co-creators with the Universe, and we don't need to work so hard! The more we allow, the less resistance we create in manifesting what we truly desire.

6. Align with your soul tribe.
   Connect with people who understand you on a soul level. This will deeply nourish you, and provide further fuel for your unique missions here on this Earth.

7. Cherish what you have.
   Cultivate deep appreciation for the blessings of your life. Know that what you have received is what you asked for, whether for joy, for growth, or simply what you need.

8. Appreciate that there is so much we do not know and will never know.
   We can't understand it all, and nor do we have to. Rest your mind from working so hard to uncover all the answers, and just enjoy the ride.

Writing Your Own Story

9. Believe in yourself.
   Back who you are and what you stand for in the world. Even if no one else does, or just one single person. Know that what you believe is your belief for a reason. Your life has meaning and a unique purpose, that only you can fulfil and transmit into the external world.

10. Enjoy the ride.
    Have fun! Embrace the humanness of life. The messy, complex unravelling of life in human form. Seek joy, new adventures and experiences. Have the time of your life!

Pearls of Wisdom:

- Our story is ours to create.
- We are the authors of our lives and it is up to us to write our own adventure.
- Life wasn't meant to be perfect, there is no such thing! Instead, it was meant to be rich, fulfilling, magical, and filled with lessons to expand our consciousness.
- Going with the flow of where your life is taking you, is so much easier than resisting the current.
- Do what makes your soul come alive, and you will never go wrong.

Writing Your Own Story

Wisdom Within:

- Do I accept who I am? What aspects of myself can I accept even more?

- Do I live my life as an authentic version of myself? Is there an area of my life in which I can more authentically speak my truth?

- What or whom do I need to let go of, to create the space to allow more of what I want to enter my life?

- What is my current soul purpose? What path is my soul yearning to follow?

- Have I surrendered to the flow of where my life is taking me? Is there an area of my life in which I could seek to surrender even more?

- Do I feel connected to the people in my life? Would I like to call in more like-minded soul connections? Is there anything I could do in the external world to bring this about?

- What am I grateful for right now in my external world? What qualities or attributes in myself am I grateful to embody?

Writing Your Own Story

- Do I tend towards over-thinking and over-analysing my life? Is it time for me to reduce or let go this pattern of thought? How might I go about doing so?

- Do I believe in myself and the dreams I have for my life? What can I do to strengthen this?

- Do I have enough joy and fun in my life? What makes me feel energised and alive? What new adventures and experiences would I like to bring into my life, to create the life that I desire?

About the Author

My greatest understanding about health and healing has come from my own journey.

It has been a series of experiences through symptoms of the body and mind, whilst simultaneously working with others going through their own, that has shed the light on what really creates dis-ease in the human body.

The body-mind-soul connection continues to expand my mind, as I have witnessed the subtleties of how conflict in the mind and soul can play out in the physical form we are blessed to inhabit. How it is rarely about the layer of the physical, and how if we truly wish to change our state of health/symptoms, we need to look at the mind, the emotions in our heart, and delve into the layers of our soul.

The medical qualifications I have obtained pale in significance to the experience of training received through the lived experience.

Dr Talia Steed

And it is my mission to expand the consciousness of medicine, to give credibility and power to others outside of the profession and modalities that have been previously looked down upon, to facilitate the ability of more and more of us to transcend our own limitations.

In the end, the journey for us all is one of awakening. That is, awakening to the ego mind, all the layers of our conditioning, and learning to move through these into a new state of being.

Every physical experience we face, every issue of the mind or heart, every encounter that triggers us, are all connected to the missions of our soul to expand into the unlimited potential, that we are.

Final Dedication

To my Mum.
For the love you showered upon me.
For the endless acts of service.
For the unwavering support.
For making me feel I always had someone to call.
For challenging me.
For triggering me to evolve more and more into a truer version of myself.
For teaching me.
For laughing with me.
For crying with me.
For never giving up on me.
For misunderstanding me and then learning to understand me.
For your love. Always your love.
I am so grateful to have you in my life and will carry you in my heart for all of my days.

www.ingramcontent.com/pod-product-compliance
Lightning Source LLC
Chambersburg PA
CBHW061221070526
44584CB00029B/3934